The Library of
NATIVE AMERICANS

The Luiseño
of California

Jack S. Williams

The Rosen Publishing Group's
PowerKids Press™
New York

For Bernard and Elizabeth Cohen, who have always supported my research

We wish to thank the Franciscan Friars of California and the friars at Mission San Luis Rey de Francia in Oceanside, California, for the use of photographs in this publication.

Published in 2003 by The Rosen Publishing Group, Inc.
29 East 21st Street, New York, NY 10010

Photo and Illustration Credits: Cover and p. 30 courtesy Jesse Peter Museum, photographs by Christine Vasquez; p. 4 Erica Clendening; pp. 7, 8 © Richard Cummins/CORBIS; pp. 10, 23 © Darrell Gulin/COR-BIS; p. 12 © Brandon D. Cole/CORBIS; pp. 14, 21, 24, 34 courtesy California Historical Society/TICOR Collection, USC Specialized Libraries and Archival Collections; pp. 17, 18, 39, 40, 43, 44, 47 courtesy Mission San Luis Rey de Francia, photographs © Christina Taccone; p. 27 © Galen Rowell/CORBIS; p. 36 © Tom Bean/CORBIS; p. 48 courtesy of the Bancroft Library, University of California, Berkeley; p. 52 © Owen Franken/CORBIS; p. 55 © Robert Holmes/CORBIS.

Book Design: Erica Clendening

Williams, Jack S.
       The Luiseño of California / Jack S. Williams.
             p. cm. — (The library of Native Americans)
       Includes bibliographical references and index.
       Contents: Introducing the Luiseños—Luiseño technology—Other features of Luiseño life—The Luiseños and the newcomers (1542–1900)—The Luiseños today.
       ISBN 0-8239-6431-0
       1. Luiseño Indians—Juvenile literature. [1. Luiseño Indians. 2. Indians of North America—California.] I. Title. II. Series.
       E99.L9 W55 2002
       979.4004'9745—dc21
                                            2002002319

Manufactured in the United States of America

Contents

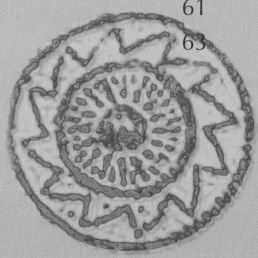

The Luiseño and Their Neighbors

Juaneño

Cahuilla

Luiseño

Ipai
(Kumyaay)

Pacific
Ocean

UNITED STATES
OF AMERICA

MEXICO

One

Introducing the Luiseños

Every night, astronomers use the massive telescope at Mount Palomar, California, to explore the most distant reaches of the universe. From the extraordinary height of 6,130 feet (570 m), the surrounding land seems to stretch out forever in all directions. These scientists may rarely think about the people who made their home on Mount Palomar in the past. However, if they could magically go back in time to 1770, they might encounter an early group of star watchers. Crouching beside campfires among the towering trees, these Native Americans also turned their eyes toward the night sky to understand their place in the universe. They told their children that some day they would die, and their spirits would become stars.

These people are called the Luiseños. The Spanish settlers gave the Native Americans the name San Luiseños because many of them lived at Mission San Luis Rey. Modern researchers have shortened the term to Luiseños. Before the mission settlement was established in 1798, the Native Americans used the names of their villages to identify themselves.

The Luiseño Nation occupied lands that stretched from Santiago Peak in the north to Agua Hedondo Creek in the south. Their home region continued into the interior of California to the first major

The Luiseño lived on the land now known as Southern California.

valleys of the coastal mountains. Because they spoke a single language, some researchers believe the Luiseños and the Native Americans who lived at Mission San Juan Capistrano were a single nation. However, the modern native peoples generally consider themselves to be separate groups. This book follows their preference and divides these Native Americans into two groups: Luiseños and Juaneños. The people of the second group usually prefer to be called Acjachemens.

No one knows when the ancestors of the Luiseños first appeared. Most experts believe that sometime between 40,000 and 13,000 years ago, human beings crossed over from Asia into North America using a frozen land bridge. Some groups of people had reached the southern end of South America by 12,000 years ago.

Most researchers believe that the ancestors of the Luiseño people came from the area that is now included in the modern state of Nevada. The Luiseño language shares many features with the Shoshone language that is still spoken by the Native Americans of that region. Many anthropologists who have studied the Luiseños believe that the group's ancestors began to move southwest about 3,500 years ago. As these ancient travelers moved their homes, they slowly replaced or mixed with older groups. Eventually, they reached the shores of the Pacific Ocean.

Many scholars believe that sometime between two and three thousand years ago, the ancestors of the Luiseños established villages on the coast of present-day southern California. Over time, these Native Americans learned how to use the wild foods of the deserts, the mountains, and the ocean. By 1400, the Luiseños had created the communities that were discovered by the Spanish explorers.

Some researchers studying this nation believe that the Luiseños are descendants of the first people who lived in California. They claim that the Luiseños have always lived in this area.

The Oceanside Pier in San Diego County, California, stands at a location where the Luiseños once fished from canoes. Much of the area that the Luiseños once lived in has been changed by modern development.

8   Scientists at Mount Palomar Observatory in San Diego County, California, observe the stars on the same spot as the Luiseños did centuries ago.

After the middle of the sixteenth century, Spanish ships began to visit the coast of southern California. Their crews occasionally traded with the natives for supplies. However, the Luiseños did not live near a place on the coast where the sailors might be tempted to stop. They probably saw fewer visitors than the other coastal native groups.

In 1769, European colonists moved into the area around San Diego. However, more than twenty years passed before the Spanish government decided to build a mission for the Luiseños. Between 1798 and 1834, Mission San Luis Rey became one of the most dramatic success stories in the history of the Americas. During the era that followed, the Native Americans faced more than a century of discrimination and hatred. Despite these challenges, the Luiseños have endured and are recognized today as one of the most remarkable native groups in California.

This book provides information about some of the important parts of the Luiseño story. It includes a basic description of the way of life of these Native Americans, as well as some of the major events that have taken place since Europeans first arrived in the Luiseño region in 1769.

Two
Luiseño Technology

The Luiseños built communities with unique characteristics. They created thousands of useful and beautiful objects from the natural resources that surrounded them. The Luiseños had a close relationship with their natural environment. Dozens of different types of animal and plant life could be found in their homeland. There were hills covered by oak forests, grasslands, cactus, and brush. Pine and cedar trees stood in the high mountains of the eastern Luiseño territory. The coast included sandy beaches and several rocky areas, as well as marshlands covered by thick stands of reeds. Fresh water was not abundant in the area where the Luiseños made their home. Because the entire area was relatively dry and hot during most of the year, the Luiseños lived near creeks and rivers.

The Native Americans used many of the plants that they found. From the land, they harvested many kinds of seeds, berries, nuts, fruits, and vegetables. The land also provided many kinds of game. Luiseño hunters brought home antelopes, bobcats, deer, elk, foxes, mice, mountain lions, rabbits, wood rats, river otters, ground squirrels, and a wide variety of insects. They ate duck and quail eggs when they could find them. Because of their religious beliefs, the Luiseños avoided eating bears, dogs,

Coyotes still hunt the hills where the Luiseños settled.

coyotes, eagles, ravens, buzzards, lizards, frogs, turtles, tree squirrels, doves, and wild pigeons.

Many different kinds of animals and plants were hunted or harvested from the ocean. The Luiseño hunted sea otters, seals, and sea lions. They also collected and ate many different kinds of shellfish, including abalone, clams, mussels, and oysters. The people gathered dozens of different kinds of sea plants, such as seaweed, and fished for crabs, bonita, and sheephead.

The Luiseños could not have survived without using many different kinds of minerals and stones. Salt was an essential item in everyone's diet. Rocks were used to create many basic tools.

Plants and trees were important sources of other raw materials.

Many of the plants and animals that the Luiseños depended on could be found year-round. However, some were only available during certain seasons. For example, acorns were particularly abundant during October and November. The

The Luiseños gathered plants from the sea to add to their diet.

Luiseños sometimes relocated their homes to temporary camps in places where food became available. In most cases, all of the food resources that were needed to survive could be found within one day's walk of their main village.

The Luiseños' ideas about nature were different from those of most Europeans. The Native Americans believed that the natural world was a living thing that should be treated with respect. When they killed an animal or cut down a tree, they often said a special prayer. The Luiseños believed that they had to balance their needs with those of other kinds of life.

Clothing and Body Decoration

The warm weather of southern California made it possible for the Luiseños to live without very much clothing. The men and children rarely covered their bodies. Every woman owned a two-piece skirt. People sometimes wore basket or reed hats. When it was wet or cold, they used robes, short capes, or blankets. Everyone wore jewelry, and most adults had some tattoos. Nearly everyone wore stout yucca sandals or deerskin shoes. Many people wore body paint on special occasions.

The Luiseño political leaders wore large capes made from bearskins or elk hide. During celebrations and rituals, the Luiseño religious leaders wore elaborate headdresses made from eagle and raven feathers. They also put on skirts and sashes made from animal hide, netting, feathers, milkweed, and grass. Other ceremonial clothing included feather cloaks and hide robes. When they went deer hunting, some men wore the stuffed heads of the animals in order to sneak up on their prey.

Villages

There were probably about fifty Luiseño villages when the Spanish colonists arrived in California in 1769. These settlements varied in size. Some included as few as fifty people, while others

had as many as 500. The average village included about 200 people. The largest communities were found on the coast.

Luiseño villages were always built near a supply of fresh water. Since most of the major settlements were found near the banks of creeks and rivers, they were often located at the bottoms of valleys in regions that had

This photo shows Luiseños living at the village of Pala during the later half of the nineteenth century (1850–1900), after the end of the mission era. Pala is one of the reservations established for Luiseño people.

hills, from where the villages could easily be defended. The houses of the village were laid out around a large, open space.

Luiseño families lived in huts made out of poles, bark, brush, or reeds. The houses were usually cone shaped. They were built inside shallow pits about 2 feet (.6 m) deep. A thick layer of soil covered some huts. They had circular floor plans. No one knows exactly how large the buildings were. Similar homes built by other coastal Native Americans ranged from 6 to 20 feet (2 to 6 m) in diameter. The families slept on blankets or reed mats with their feet pointed toward a hearth, or fire pit, in the middle of the room. A small opening was left in the center of the roof. This hole allowed sunlight into the structure and made it possible for smoke to escape. When it rained or snowed, a piece of hide was used to cover the opening. Some houses had a short tunnel that served as the entrance. A person had to crawl on his or her hands and knees to enter these houses. The Luiseño families kept most of their possessions inside their homes.

All Luiseño houses had one or more granaries. These small structures were used to store acorns and other seeds that were to be eaten during the winter. The granaries looked like large baskets elevated above the ground on boulders or wooden poles.

Based on similar California Native American settlements, anthropologists believe that most Luiseño villages also included a larger home that was reserved for the use of the chief, or community political leader. Most of the extra space inside these structures was used for storage.

Every village had at least one sweat lodge. These buildings were similar to the Luiseño homes, except they were built in deeper pits. Inside the structure, a fire produced billowing smoke and strong heat. Thick layers of mud covered the insides and outsides of the walls. The smoke slowly escaped through a small hole in the roof. In order to get in and out of the building, the Luiseños crawled through a small doorway. The sweat lodges were used for religious cleansing and healing. After people had been inside the structure for a while, they used deer ribs or curved sticks to scrape away their sweat.

Many people followed their visit to the sweat lodge with a swim in a nearby creek or river. The Luiseños also set up various kinds of rectangular pole-and-brush coverings for shade. During the day, both men and women sat in the shelter of these structures while they worked.

In the middle of most villages, there was a *wámkish*. This was a large, circular area used for worship, surrounded by a wooden or brush fence. Inside this sacred space, the religious leaders set up a kind of table with a sacred statue or image made of animal skin and feathers. Many different kinds of ceremonies took place in front of the *wámkish*.

The Luiseños burned their dead and buried the remains in ceramic urns. When someone passed away, most of what that person owned was burned so that he or she could use it in the afterlife.

Cooking

The Luiseño women used many different cooking methods. When the weather permitted, the meals were prepared outdoors. They roasted some kinds of food over an open flame. Other items were smoked, using slow-burning fires. The cooks also used steam to prepare meals. Several types of wild plants, such as acorns and buckeyes, had to be ground into a fine powder and then soaked in fresh water to remove natural poisons. Some kinds of shellfish,

Manos, *metates*, pestles, and mortars were used to pulverize foods in order to prepare them to be eaten. The *metate* in the upper left hand corner was imported from Mexico during the mission period (1769–1835).

such as abalone, had to be tenderized before it was cooked. Many of the wild plants, such as cactus fruit, could be eaten without any preparation.

Some Luiseño dishes were prepared in pits. These ovens consisted of large holes that were dug into the ground. A fire was built in the pits. Large stones were slowly added to the flames. When the stones were red hot, poles were used to drag them out of the hole. Some of the stones were put back into the pit along with food, such as shellfish or meat, that had been wrapped in leaves or clay. The remaining hot rocks and earth were piled on top of the oven. After a few hours, the foods could be served.

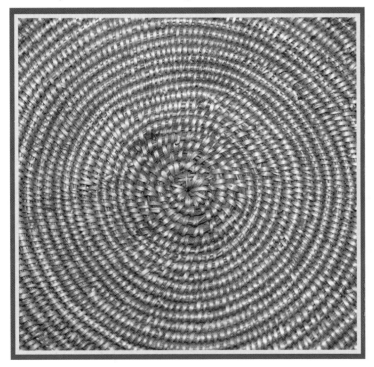

The Luiseños prepared their meals using a combination of pottery, stone bowls, and tightly-woven baskets. In order to cook in a basket, they placed heated stones into liquid mixtures, such as a stew or soup. The

The Luiseños prepared meals in tightly-woven baskets.

cooks had to be careful to keep stirring the contents or the stones would burn a hole in the container. A similar technique was used to prepare seeds and nuts. Small pieces of burning wood were tossed onto woven or ceramic trays, along with the food. The trays had to be constantly shaken or the glowing wood fragments would cause the seeds, nuts, or trays to burn.

Many types of berries were crushed to make drinks. Other plants were boiled to produce a kind of tea. These drinks were served as both medicine and refreshments.

Some items could be preserved for later use. Fish and meat were often salted and smoked. The fruits and vegetables that were not eaten immediately were dried in the sun.

Arts and Crafts

The early Luiseños produced an amazing variety of objects. Many of the items that have survived show that the Luiseños were extraordinary artists and craftspeople.

Like most other early Native Americans, the Luiseños found that stone was one of their most important resources. They created dozens of different types of chipped stone tools, such as arrowheads, drills, knives, and spear points. These tools were made for cutting, drilling, scraping, prying, and dozens of other uses. Some of the harder types of stone were ground into other types of tools. For example, every community had dozens of mortars and pestles. Pestles are a kind of long stone cylinder. They were used with rocks that had large, round holes. These bowl-like stones were called mortars. The Luiseños also ground harder types of stones into *manos*, which were fist-sized pieces of rock that looked like bars of soap. The *manos* were used with *metates*, which were flat or shallow bowl-shaped slabs of stone. Pestles, mortars, *manos*, and *metates* were used to crack and grind nuts and seeds, such as acorns. Other stone objects that were made by grinding include arrow-shaft straighteners, ritual bowls, beads, anchors, and smoking pipes.

The Luiseños were also experts in making pottery. They created their ceramic products using clay that they dug out of streambeds and hillsides. In order to construct a vessel, the potters combined the dry clay with sand and water. The mixture was then formed into long, cigar-shaped pieces. The solid clay tubes were coiled together until the vessel was completed. The surface of the pot was then smoothed with a round stone and wooden paddle. A few potters decorated their vessels by painting lines, or carving them using a stick or fingernail. After the ceramic objects had completely dried, they were stacked together with tree bark, or a similar fuel, in a shallow pit. The pile of pots and fuel was then set on fire. After many hours of burning, the pottery was allowed to cool. Most of the Luiseños' ceramics were used to cook or to store food. The forms that were popular included bowls, ladles, plates, trays, and jars. A special kind of pot with two mouths was used as a water jar. The Luiseños also made tube-shaped ceramic beads and pipes.

Many minerals were transformed into other useful raw materials. Naturally-occurring tar was collected from the beaches and was used as a kind of glue. Carbon was used to make black paint.

The Luiseños were able to make many useful things from the animals they hunted. Hides were used to make skirts, bags, blankets, quivers, robes, shoes, and pouches. Bones were made into beads, earrings, fish-hooks, gambling sticks, hammers, musical instruments, nose plugs, needles, sweat sticks, and many other tools. Bear claws were used as beads and pendants. Feathers were used to decorate arrows, capes, dance skirts, head-dresses and robes. Seashells became fish-hooks and jewelry. Turtle shells and deer hooves were transformed into rattles and pendants. The brains of some animals, such as deer, were used to tan hides. Sinew, a kind of muscle, was taken from the bodies of dead deer and combined with wood to make powerful bows.

This photo shows a Cahuilla woman creating a basket. Similar methods were used to make Luiseño baskets. The Cahuilla are close relatives of the Luiseños.

Plants were also an important source for raw materials. Grass, yucca, rushes, and aromatic sumac were collected and woven into baskets by Luiseño women and girls. The baskets were decorated with a combination of darker tan, black, or brown geometric designs. Dozens of different types of baskets were made, including bowls, fish traps, hats, jars, seed beaters, sifters, and trays. Wood and cane were used to make arrows, balls for sports, canoe paddles, clubs, cradle boards, digging sticks, fish traps, house beams, musical instruments, nose plugs, poles, snares, spears, stirring sticks, throwing sticks, tongs, and many other objects.

Wood and basketry were combined to make other useful things, such as fish traps. The Luiseños learned to catch fish using poisonous plants. Tobacco and similar plants were smoked during religious rituals. Soaproot was used as a kind of glue, a poison, or as a raw material to make brushes. Greasewood produced another kind of glue. Cedar bark and cottonwood bark were transformed into cloth. Yucca, milkweed, hemp, nettles, and similar plants were made into strings, cords, ropes, slings, shoes, bags, capes, fishnets, rabbit nets, pouches, robes, and many other similar objects. Dried gourds were fashioned into rattles.

The Luiseños used reed canoes, called *tule balsas*, to fish and to travel along the coast. They tied together many cigar-shaped bundles of reeds together to build a canoe. The vessels were about

10 feet (3 m) long and about 3 feet (1 m) wide. They could hold up to four people. Some Luiseños also fashioned tree trunks into similar, small dugout canoes. The crews equipped the canoes with wooden paddles and stone anchors.

The yucca plant was used by the Luiseño in order to make many useful objects.

Three

Other Features of Luiseño Life

Scholars recognize that the people we call Luiseños and their close relatives, the Acjachemens, shared certain features of language, social structure, government, warfare, trade, and religion. These traits were generally similar to those of the groups that surrounded them on the north and east, but were strikingly different from those of the Kumyaay Native Americans to the south.

Language

The Luiseños spoke a language that was similar to the Serranos, Acjachemens, Cahuillas, Cupeños, and Tongva. Of these peoples, the Acjachemens spoke a language that was most similar to that of the Luiseños. Although there were some minor local differences, all Acjachemens and Luiseños could easily communicate with each other.

Social Structure

A community's social structure provides a way of dividing people into smaller groups. Among the Luiseños, individuals were assigned to a group based on age, birthplace, gender, and their

The Cahuilla father and son shown here during the second half of the nineteenth century (1850–1900) shared many aspects of life with the early Luiseños. Before 1900, the Native Americans had also adopted many characteristics of European culture, including western-style clothing.

fathers' social status. A person's place in society was also determined by how much power that person, and his or her family, had.

The smallest Luiseño social unit was the family. The work that family members were assigned was usually determined by age and if they were men or women. Compared to other Native American groups, Luiseño adults had a considerable amount of freedom to choose what their jobs were. For example, some men cooked, and some women hunted.

One of the most important groups for males was the warrior society. Members had to go through a special set of rituals to join. The warriors played a special part in Luiseño society by protecting and defending the community from outsiders.

A chief, who was known as the *nó't*, ruled each settlement. This position was usually handed down from father to son. A set of assistants, known as the *paxá*, and a council of village elders and religious leaders aided the chiefs. Each of these men inherited their positions from their fathers or uncles. The rulers were given many privileges. The *nó't* was allowed to have two wives. He also received the food that was produced on community-owned lands. However, most of these materials were returned to the villagers during religious ceremonies or were used to entertain guests from other communities.

Every Luiseño village represented a kind of group called a clan. The members believed that their founding father was an animal, such as a bear or an eagle. Besides the members of the Luiseño clans, there were also a small number of slaves found living in the villages. Children and young women from enemy groups who were captured during wars became the property of individuals and families. They had to work hard for their masters, or they could be severely punished or killed.

Most of the Luiseño spiritual leaders were men. They were believed to have special abilities that could be used for both good and evil. The spiritual leaders knew many secret rituals, dances, and songs that were

The bear was a founding animal for a Luiseño clan.

supposed to have the power to make people well or sick. These people were always respected, and sometimes feared.

Government

The basic unit of government of the Luiseños was the village. Anthropologists sometimes call these small communities tribelets. Although each village maintained its own treaties with other communities, there was an overall system of political leadership that was provided by a few senior ruling families. These families could be found in every settlement, and they were the ones who almost always guided community life.

Each Luiseño village had its own territory, where its people had the right to hunt and gather. These lands were divided into those owned by individuals, those owned by families, and those owned by the community as a whole. Anyone else who wanted to come into these areas had to get permission. Many of the groups that lived away from the ocean owned smaller areas of the coast, where they would come each year to fish, hunt, and gather. These owners carefully marked the different land units.

Every Luiseño settlement had its village chief, the *nó't*. These men organized and supervised community work efforts and religious ceremonies. During times of war, they served as military leaders. Compared to their neighbors, the *nó'ts* had an unusual amount of power over the lives of their people.

Warfare

Warfare was an important part of Luiseño life. The native warriors' main weapon was a powerful longbow that was 5 feet (1.5 m) tall. A quiver was slung over the shoulder that held a fistful of arrows. Other war tools included clubs, thrusting spears, javelins, and slings. The Luiseño women worked to create provisions for military expeditions and often accompanied the warriors when they marched off to combat. The fighters decorated their bodies with dramatic painted designs.

Wars were fought for a variety of reasons. Some conflicts involved competition over natural resources, such as fishing and gathering areas. Other struggles developed out of accusations of witchcraft or trespassing. The Luiseños rarely fought with each other or the Acjachemens. However, they sometimes made war on other nearby, Shoshone-speaking peoples, such as the Cahuilla. They were almost always at war with the Kumyaay villagers to their south.

Much of Luiseño warfare focused on raids. Once a reason for war was established, groups of young warriors would invade enemy territory and capture or kill anyone they found. Enemy men and women were usually slaughtered on the spot, but the younger women and children were carried off as slaves. The victors would return with prisoners and stolen items for celebrations. If they had a chance, the Luiseños would sometimes destroy whole villages.

Games

Even though they had to work hard, the Luiseños still liked to play many different kinds of games. Some of the recreational events were similar to modern sports, like hockey. In some villages, there was a large, flat, open area with a smooth surface that was set aside for sports contests. In one game, the two teams tried to score points using sticks and a wooden ball. Other games used painted wooden dice and similar game pieces made from rawhide and bone. Whenever people gathered in large groups, they usually found time to play.

This magnificent basket from the Jesse Peter Museum demonstrates the Luiseños' ability to create items that were both beautiful and functional.

Religion

The early Luiseños had a complex set of beliefs that provided them with a way to make sense of their lives and to figure out what they needed to do to be good people. The ceremonies were often filled with dramas and storytelling. These memorized stories were told in an ancient language that very few of the Luiseños understood. There were dozens of different kinds of ceremonies. Each had its own leaders and purposes.

The Luiseños' way of thinking about the structure of the universe was very different from that of most modern Americans. They believed that Wiyót, who was the son of Mother Earth, created the universe. He was responsible for the formation of the world known to the Luiseño, including its plants, animals, and people.

One of the most important of the Luiseños' stories involved the sacred being known as Chingichngish. He was the most powerful force in the universe. Chingichngish established nearly all of the Luiseño customs and rules. Unless he remained happy with his people, terrible things could happen. According to his rules, everyone must respect their elders, share food, follow their leaders' orders, avoid anger, and be polite to their relatives. If you did what was right, you were rewarded with good health and a wonderful afterlife.

Nearly all the Luiseño holidays involved their religion. There were rituals for every stage in a person's life. There were especially important ceremonies marking the adulthood of men and women. Other religious celebrations marked the passing seasons. The festivals usually involved dancing and songs. Voices, flutes, rattles, and whistles provided the music. Split pieces of wood, called clapper sticks, were used to snap out a rhythm. Craftsmen tied string to the end of a piece of wood to make a bullroarer. When the musician spun the bullroarer in the air, it hummed loudly.

The men usually performed the sacred dances and led the ceremonies. The women participated by singing and preparing food. The religious leaders sometimes wore special clothing and paint that made them look like animals or supernatural beings. They had many special sacred tools, including clay figures of people, special bowls for making ritual drinks, stone smoking pipes, wooden wands decorated with stones and shells, dance skirts, feather headdresses, special minerals and stones, swallowing sticks, and various kinds of tubes.

Many individuals and families had their own sets of rituals, sacred songs, and knowledge. These ideas were handed down to their children and were rarely shared with other members of the community or outsiders.

During some sacred ceremonies, the Luiseño religious leaders created complex pictures on the ground using sand. Most of the images were linked to Chingichngish. Other paintings showed the Luiseño universe, other sacred people, and sometimes a person who had died.

Some Luiseños marked the surface of rocks with symbols or other signs. This kind of display is known as rock art. Sometimes they used paint to mark the rocks. These pictures are called pictographs. Other symbols were created by scraping away some of the rocks' outer surface. This kind of picture is called a petroglyph. Many scholars think that these images were made during religious rituals. Because rock art is sacred to many modern Native Americans, it is very important that people show respect when they view pictographs and petroglyphs.

Four

The Luiseños and the Europeans (1542–1900)

Juan Rodriguez Cabrillo was the first European to explore the coastline of southern California. Some Luiseños probably glimpsed his ships in October 1542. However, Cabrillo and other explorers and merchants who came to the region between 1542 and 1769 did not record any visits with the Luiseños. No one knows for sure what happened to the Native Americans during this long period of time. Throughout most of the New World, Europeans introduced ferocious diseases that may have killed as many as 95 percent of the native population. Given the frequent visits of the Spaniards to other parts of California, it is likely that diseases spread to the Luiseño communities, and many people probably died. By the time the Spaniards came to stay in nearby areas in 1769, the population had probably decreased, and then increased, as it had in most of North America.

The Luiseños and the Missions

During the middle of the eighteenth century, several European powers fought for the control of North America. King Carlos III of Spain heard rumors that the English and the Russians were trying to

This photograph of a Cahuilla Native American family in front of their home was taken during the late nineteenth century. The Luiseños and the Cahuillas underwent similar changes during this period. Both groups gradually adopted the dress and tools of newcomers from other parts of the United States.

extend their rule to the lands that bordered the Pacific Ocean. At the time, Spain owned these lands. Spain feared losing California. If California was taken, its harbors could be used to attack Mexico and Peru, the two regions that were the richest parts of the Spanish Empire. In 1769, Carlos sent an expedition to occupy California.

In order to create a colony, the Spanish government depended on a combination of military bases and missions. The military bases served as homes for small groups of soldiers and settlers. The army was sent to prevent other countries from capturing California.

Why did Spain establish missions? King Carlos III wanted to control California. However, he did not have the colonists, the money, or the soldiers that were needed to conquer the region. The only way that the king's officials could secure California was to create some kind of friendship with the Native Americans who lived there. The king's

Flowers bloom around a memorial to explorer Juan Rodriguez Cabrillo on San Miguel Island. Cabrillo was probably on this island during his explorations of the California coast in 1542. He is believed to be buried here, although his gravesite has not been discovered.

advisors decided that missions would be used to colonize the remote region. These settlements would be built as communities where Native Americans would gradually be transformed into Spanish citizens. The government selected a group of Franciscan priests, headed by Junípero Serra, to lead this dangerous and difficult task.

Many Franciscans were anxious to go to California. They believed that their work in the province would provide them with an opportunity to share their belief in God and to help the Native Americans, whom they viewed as poor people. The Franciscans were also glad to serve their nation. They hoped that they would be able to build missions that combined the best things found in the European and the Native American worlds.

Living on the Edge of a Mission Frontier

In 1769, a Spanish expedition headed by Gaspar de Portolá reached the Luiseño region. They had no idea how they would be treated by the local Native Americans. The Spaniards were pleased by the natives' friendly manners and their willingness to trade. After passing through the region, the Spanish colonists continued on their way to found the capital of the province in central California. After two key military bases had been established in the south at San Diego and in the north at Monterey, new missions were gradually established along the coastline. These outposts were much more than churches with a few priests. Each settlement was also a kind of government agency meant to introduce the Native Americans to the Spanish way of life, including a whole range of new ideas, animals, plants, and tools.

For the missionaries to succeed, they had to persuade Native Americans to join the new communities. Why would someone want to move into a mission? A person who lived in the new settlements enjoyed a number of practical benefits. The foreigners brought steel axes, knives, dozens of new kinds of food, and animals such as cattle, chickens, horses, mules, and sheep. The missionaries also had many things of beauty, including paintings, statues, religious rituals, and music. The Spanish soldiers brought powerful weapons, such as firearms and steel swords.

Some Native Americans were probably attracted to the missions because of the Franciscans' preaching. Many of the Franciscans were visionaries, who offered the native peoples a chance to build a new kind of utopia, or perfect world. We have no way of knowing how many of the native people were attracted by the priests' ideals.

The Franciscans called the Native Americans who decided to live at the missions neophytes, or new followers. Many village leaders brought their whole communities to the new settlements. After they had moved, the elders often continued to serve as leaders. The neophytes were allowed to visit and trade with non-Christian natives, whom the Spaniards called gentiles. The neophytes sometimes persuaded their gentile relatives to return and live with them in the missions.

Though the Europeans and missionaries occupied California for a long time, they rarely interacted with the Luiseños. In 1775, a mission was built to the north for the Tongva Nation in what is today the Los Angeles area. Four years later, another Franciscan outpost was added about halfway between Los Angeles and San Diego at San Juan Capistrano. The Native Americans who lived there were the Acjachemens, the close relatives of the Luiseños.

Between 1776 and 1798, many of the Luiseños visited the new missions, especially San Juan Capistrano. However, most of these Native Americans decided not to leave their old villages. Some of the Luiseños traded with their neighbors

Shown in this photo is Father Jeremiah Joseph O'Keefe, the Franciscan priest who was probably most responsible for the restoration of Mission San Luis Rey. Father O'Keefe worked at the site between 1892 and 1912. This photo was probably taken around 1893.

for European-style goods, such as cloth, glass beads, and steel knives. Luiseños liked the taste of beef, lamb, and chicken, as well as the foods made from the grains and vegetables that the Europeans brought. Some natives began to plant the same crops as the newcomers. A few of the Luiseños even started to raise European animals, such as chickens and sheep.

Long after the mission period had ended (1769–1835), the United States government encouraged the creation of residential schools for Native Americans where they were treated with great cruelty. A few groups of Catholic clergy continued to teach natives using more humane methods.

A Mission for the Luiseños

As the years passed, the Luiseños watched Mission San Juan Capistrano become a prosperous place. At some Franciscan settlements, Native Americans rejected the newcomers. Fighting between Spanish soldiers and Kumyaay warriors was common to the south of the Luiseño country within the territory of the San Diego Mission. In the San Francisco region, far to the north of the Luiseños, many neophytes decided to run away. However, these problems did not become important at San Juan because most of the natives seemed to have supported the mission, and very few people tried to leave.

Meanwhile, the Luiseño community leaders began to face serious problems. The newcomers' horses, sheep, and cattle quickly multiplied. The animals ate traditional crops and disrupted nearly all aspects of the natural environment. It became almost impossible for the Luiseños to live off the land as they once had. At the same time, many villagers expressed interest in more trade goods. The Luiseños also continued their long war with the Kumyaay people to the south. They needed allies. Some leaders believed that if the Luiseños had their own mission, it would make them more powerful and their people more prosperous.

In 1795, the Spanish government was finally ready to establish a mission for the Luiseños. After a series of explorations were made, the village of Quechla was selected for the new outpost. The settlement was dedicated in 1798, to Saint Louis, or San Luis, the king of France, with much fanfare by Father President Fermín Lasuén. Among the priests who were present was a young man from the region of Spain known as Catalonia, who was named Antonio Peyri. Father Peyri was one of the two priests who were assigned to live at the outpost. Between 1798 and 1832, he remained at San Luis Rey, building one of the most remarkable relationships with Native Americans seen in the history of California.

The work at the new mission proceeded at an amazing pace. A group of Luiseños who had moved to Mission Santa Bárbara returned to help with the first phase of the project. Unlike other missions, the neophytes and the Franciscans seemed to have understood and respected each other from the start. Working together, the Franciscans and the Native Americans replaced the first log-and-grass buildings with more permanent structures. Soon they were turning out hundreds of thousands of tons of earthen building blocks, tiles, and cement. Large areas of the land surrounding the river became productive fields and gardens. Herds of sheep, cattle, horses, and mules covered the grassy hillsides. All the people of the missions shared in the work, the community's products, and its harvests.

Over time, it became obvious that there were not enough resources for all the neophytes and livestock at, or near, Mission San Luis Rey. Consequently, Father Peyri decided to bring the benefits of the mission to the Native Americans, where they had traditionally lived. He negotiated the right to create ranches, farms, and churches in at least nine of the existing gentile settlements, including San Antonio de Pala; San Pedro, or Las Flores; San Juan, or Guajome; Agua Caliente; Santa Margarita; San Onofre; San Jacinto; Temecula; and San Marcos. The settlements were organized into four districts: Quechla, Pala, Temeku, and Usva. A council of seven Christian Native American mayors, headed by a captain general, helped Peyri to govern the Christian Luiseños living throughout the region, which now included more than 1,000 square miles (2,590 km). Peyri gave the older village leaders who were Christians the title of captain and allowed them to keep many of their privileges outside of the government. The older community councils of elders also continued to exist.

In keeping with the Franciscans' rules, the Luiseño villagers at the remote outposts were not forced to become Christians. Instead, the religions and customs of both the Luiseño and the Europeans existed side by side. Not all the Luiseño villages had neophytes. Some Native American communities were not

At Mission San Luis Rey de Francia, priests and Native Americans developed an extraordinary and productive relationship.

included in the mission system. However, even these gentiles seem to have accepted the fact that some of their relatives were Christians. The region remained at peace.

The population of the neophytes continued to rise as more of the Luiseños decided to become Christians. By the end of the mission era in 1834, there were nearly 3,000 Native Americans listed at Mission San Luis Rey, making it the largest single Christian community in California.

By the end of the mission period, it was also obvious that many

Luiseños had mastered the skills they had learned from the Europeans. They routinely erected magnificent buildings and practiced many Spanish trades. The main building complex of the mission measured 600 by 450 feet (182 by 136 m). It was the largest man-made structure in California.

Although many changes had taken place since 1798, it was clear

This photo shows the interior of a priest's room at Mission San Luis Rey de Francia.

that the Luiseños had not forgotten or given up many of their old customs and beliefs. Most neophytes mastered the new ways but preserved what they valued in their old traditions, including their language, sports, dances, and many religious stories and beliefs. Although they learned many new customs from the Spanish settlers, they were still living under their own leaders, in a largely native world.

The End of the Missions

In 1822, the California settlements received word that Spain had abandoned its claim to California. A year earlier, Mexican rebels had won their war for independence. California and the Native Americans who lived in the missions were now part of the new nation of Mexico.

Political leaders sent from the south promised the neophytes that they would soon be given complete control of the mission towns and other property. Many Luiseño leaders probably felt that they were ready to take their place in the new society of Mexico. The Franciscan missionaries had promised them from the start that someday they would leave and would give the natives complete control of their lands and property. However, by 1824, the church officials were convinced that the talk of freedom for the neophytes was simply an excuse for greedy ranchers to grab control of the Native Americans' land and other possessions. For years, settlers in California had complained that they deserved the best lands and that the Native Americans were being given special benefits.

Elsewhere in California, the new political changes and conflicts created hard feelings that led to violence. In 1824, the Chumash missions were torn apart in a bloody revolt. In 1826, some of the Luiseño native leaders were granted additional rights to self-government by Governor José María Echeandía. However, the entire region was soon plunged into a series of civil wars fought between the various groups of settlers and the central government of Mexico. In 1828, Estanislao, a Native American mayor from Mission San José, tried to create his own state in the Sierra Nevada Mountains. It was a time of chaos, and in the end the Luiseños' rights and property were lost to the greed of the newcomers.

Father Peyri, who had for so long hoped that things would get better, finally decided that the best thing that he could do was leave. In 1832, the old priest departed with two young Luiseño boys. Together, they journeyed to Rome, where he saw to it that the young Native Americans were enrolled in studies that would lead to their becoming priests. Peyri believed that these boys would return to serve their people, something that he felt he could no longer do.

Pablo Tac, one of the two boys, wrote a short history of his life at Mission San Luis Rey. It provides some of our only insights into the Native Americans' way of looking at the missions. His writing makes it clear that life in the mission was filled with happiness and challenges. He was clearly grateful for the work of the Franciscans, especially Father Peyri. Sadly, both of the young men who were sent to Rome died before they could return to their homeland.

The Luiseños
After the Mission Experience

In 1834, the Mexican government finally decreed the end of the missions. A few individual Luiseño leaders received land grants. Attempts were made to establish Luiseño towns at Las Flores and Santa Margarita. However, greedy ranchers soon stole most of the natives' properties. The Luiseños were left with few choices. Some became cowboys or servants. Others were captured and forced to live as slaves. A few Luiseños tried to go back to their old ways. Some mission settlements, such as Pala and San Luis Rey, were

During the period after the missions were closed, life grew more difficult for the Luiseños.

never completely abandoned. Loyal Luiseños continued to do what they could to keep up the churches and other places of worship.

Some of the former neophytes escaped to the east and joined with other hostile Native American peoples. They helped to organize raiding parties that captured thousands of cattle and horses from the Mexican ranches. By 1845, it looked as if the Native Americans might drive the newcomers out of California.

Everything changed dramatically in 1846. The Mexican-American War broke out, ending in a 1848 treaty that made the region a part of the United States. The Luiseños quickly discovered that the new

This 1827 etching by Auguste Duhaut-Cilly depicts Mission San Luis Rey.

government was no friendlier than that of Mexico. The United States Army quickly crushed any Native American resistance. Most of the United States's political leaders believed that all of California's native peoples should be eliminated or sent away. The gold rush of 1849 brought other changes. Within a few years, tens of thousands of newcomers from all over the world moved to California. They rapidly settled on most of the remaining open lands that had once belonged to Native Americans.

The Luiseños found it difficult to deal with the new invaders. Although the Republic of Mexico had not treated them with fairness, the mission's Native Americans had been made citizens with the same rights as everyone else. The new government of the United States denied nearly all Native Americans their basic rights as human beings. In 1850, the governor of California went so far as to order a war of extermination against the remaining native peoples. Laws were issued that made it possible for government officials to imprison poor Native Americans and to make them work for free. In 1853, Bishop Joseph Alemany tried to get the federal government to recognize the Christian Native Americans' right to the mission lands. However, the U.S. Supreme Court rejected the claim.

In 1875, some of the remote Luiseño communities, including Pala, Potrero, La Jolla, and Yapiche, were given a special status as a kind of semi-reservation. Most of the Native Americans were left without land. In 1891, the Act for the Relief of Mission Indians established reservations at La Jolla, Rincón, Pauma, Pechanga, Pala, and Soboba. The majority of government officials, teachers, doctors, and nurses were sent to these areas. In the decades that followed, the Luiseños partially took over the role of keeping law and order on the reservations.

The new reservation system provided some help, but created additional hardships for the Luiseños. Their children were forced to attend schools where they were taught that Native American ways of doing things were stupid or evil. Government officials, who were Protestants, also insisted that most of their Roman Catholic beliefs were backward or bad. The children were forced to speak English and to adopt the same customs as the Protestant Americans of European descent. Although they were allowed to vote for certain native leaders within their communities, the government required that their American representatives approved them.

Much of the daily life of the Luiseños on their reservations continued to echo the activities of the mission era. The Luiseños worked as farmers and ranchers. They occasionally sought work off the reservations as laborers. The natives undertook some activities, such as hunting and gathering, when they could.

Other Luiseños who lived away from the reservations continued their own struggle to be treated with fairness and dignity. By the end of the nineteenth century, most of the remaining Luiseños who lived in places such as San Juan Capistrano and

Oceanside, realized that as long as they said that they were Native Americans, they would not be given any civil rights. Most of the survivors who lived outside the reservations told the government officials that they were Mexican-Americans. Although Mexicans were not treated fairly by the government, they were not treated as badly as were the Native Americans.

Five

The Luiseños Today

The Luiseños have never given up their struggle for civil rights and the preservation of their culture. Although they were not yet given the right to vote, many Native Americans served as soldiers in World War I. In 1919, the Mission Indian Federation was formed as a way of carrying the Luiseños' protests to government officials. In 1924, the reservation groups were finally given the right to vote. In 1934, the Luiseño communities rejected the Indian Reorganization Act because it did not give them the right to govern themselves. In World War II, Native American men went to war for a second time for the United States. Despite the setbacks, government involvement on the reservations continued to create desperately needed jobs and education opportunities. Little by little, things slowly improved.

By 1950, the reservation school systems that had hurt so many native children were finally eliminated. The adults who lived on the reservations were taking a greater role in their self-government. New programs that were designed to increase the number of jobs and to improve the quality of life in the Luiseño communities were started. Native American leaders took on important roles in state and county Native American organizations, such as the Intertribal Council of California.

Native Americans, including the Luiseños, have fought in several American wars. In this photo, American veterans salute during the anniversary of the D-Day invasion, which occurred during World War II.

The Luiseños continue to preserve their identity as proud Native Americans. As with other peoples, their culture continues to grow and change. More than 90 percent of the known members of the nation consider themselves to be Roman Catholics. Many Luiseños also practice traditional Native American religious customs.

No one knows how many descendants of this nation are alive today. In 1990, 1,795 people lived on the reservations. The Luiseños have continued their struggle to preserve their sacred places and objects. Some groups are fighting for the return of parts of their lost homeland. Along with many other Native American groups, the Luiseños are very angry about the way that their ancestors' remains have been treated in the past. They want universities and museums to return their tribal property.

The Luiseños have an amazing heritage. Their ancestors created a world of plenty that lasted for hundreds of years. They found a peaceful way of dealing with the changes brought about by the repeated invasions of their homeland. Luiseños deserve to be treated with respect and recognized for the important part that they have played in the larger story of America.

By showing respect for Luiseño homeland and artifacts, we respect Luiseño heritage. This photo is of Mount Shasta, a traditional Luiseño site in Montague, California.

55

Timeline

13,000– 40,000 years ago	Luiseños' ancestors arrive in North America from Asia.
3,500 years ago	Most scholars believe that the Shoshone speakers, who are the ancestors of the Luiseños, begin the long migration to the south and west.
2,500 years ago	Most scholars believe that the Shoshone speakers arrive on the coast of Southern California. These people are probably the ancestors of the later Luiseño Nation.
1400	The Luiseños are living in villages that will eventually be discovered by Europeans.
1542	Juan Rodriguez Cabrillo's ships pass by the Luiseños' territory.
1769	Spanish colonists invade California and visit the Luiseños.
1775	A mission is established near San Juan Capistrano.

1798	Mission San Luis Rey, established for the Luiseños, is dedicated.
1821	Mexico becomes independent of Spain. The Luiseños become citizens of the new nation.
1835	Mission San Luis Rey is taken over by administrators appointed by the Mexican government. During the next decade, nearly all the Luiseño lands are lost.
1848	The United States wins the Mexican-American War and takes control of California. Native Americans lose their status as citizens.
1850–1875	Laws are passed that deny civil rights to Native Americans.
1875	Semi-reservations are created for some Luiseños at Pala, Potrero, La Jolla, and Yapiche.
1891	The Act for the Relief of Mission Indians establishes formal reservations for some Luiseños.
1924	All Native Americans are made U.S. citizens.
1960–present	Many Luiseños become involved in the Native American civil rights movement.

Glossary

anthropologists (an-thruh-PAH-luh-jists)   Scholars who study cultural, social, and physical aspects of human life.

astronomy (uh-STRAH-nuh-mee)   The study of stars and other types of bodies found outside of Earth's atmosphere.

aqueduct (AK-wuh-duhkt)   A man-made channel used to carry water.

chief (CHEEF)   A kind of leader who receives special privileges and who collects goods, which he redistributes among his people.

clan (KLAN)   A group of families that claim to be related to the same animal ancestor.

clapper sticks (KLA-puhr STIKS)   A kind of musical instrument that was used to beat out rhythm.

culture (KUHL-chur)   The shared, learned behavior of a group of people living together.

dugout (DUG-owt)   A kind of canoe made by hollowing out a log.

gentile (JEN-tyl)   A word used for non-Christian Native Americans under Spanish rule.

hearth (HARTH)   A pit used for fires.

manos (MAH-nohs)   Fist-sized pieces of stone used to grind seeds on a metate.

metates (meh-TAH-tays)   Stone slabs with a bowl-like depressions used with a *mano.*

mission (MIH-shuhn)   In precolonial and colonial California, a Spanish religious settlement where Native Americans were to be taught to live as Christian citizens.

mortars (MOR-turz)   Circular holes in rocks that were used to crack nuts and to grind seeds into flour.

neophytes (NEE-oh-fyts)   A term used for mission Native Americans who were new followers of the Christian religion.

nó't (NOH-aht)   A Luiseño term for village leader, or chief.

paxá (pa-HAH)   A Luiseño term for an assistant to the chief.

pendant (PEN-duhnt)   A type of jewelry suspended on a cord worn around the neck.

pestles (PES-tuhls)   Cylindrical-shaped pieces of rocks used with mortars.

petroglyphs (PEH-truh-glihfs)   Rock art that is created by pecking the outer surface off of rocks.

pictographs (PIK-tuh-grafs)   Rock art that is created by scraping images onto rock surfaces.

rock art (RAHK ART)   An art tradition that involves painting and pecking decorations and symbols on the surface of rocks.

sinew (SIN-yoo)   A kind of muscle used to make bows.

social structure (SOH-shul STRUHK-chur)   A way of dividing a community into different groups of people.

tule balsa (TOO-lee BAL-suh)   A kind of canoe made from bundles of reeds.

utopia (yoo-TOH-pee-uh)   A kind of ideal community where everyone is happy and is treated fairly.

wámkish (WAHM-keesh)   A sacred area in the middle of the village used for worship.

Resources

BOOKS

Campbell, Paul. *Survival Skills of Native California*. Salt Lake City, UT: Gibbs Smith, 1999.

Malinowski, Sharon (editor). *Gale Encyclopedia of Native American Tribes* (volume three). Detroit, MI: Gale Group, 1998.

MUSEUMS

Mission San Luis Rey de Francia
4050 Mission Avenue
Oceanside, CA 92068
(760) 757-3651

San Antonio de Pala
Pala Mission Road
Pala, CA 92059
(760) 742-1600

Temecula Valley Museum
28315 Mercedes Street
Temecula, CA 92590
(909) 694-6452

WEB SITES

Due to the changing nature of Internet links, PowerKids Press has developed an online list of Web sites related to the subject of this book. This site is updated regularly. Please use this link to access the site:

www.powerkidslinks.com/lna/luiseno

Index